EXMOOR
VOLUME 2

Walk Footpaths and Bridleways ... Rest by Clear Sparkling Waters

Shirley and Mike Hesman

First published in Great Britain in 2014

Copyright text and photographs © 2014 Shirley and Mike Hesman

British Library Cataloguing-in-Publication Data
A CIP record for this title is available from the British Library

ISBN 978 0 85710 087 0

PiXZ Books
Halsgrove House, Ryelands Business Park,
Bagley Road, Wellington, Somerset TA21 9PZ
Tel: 01823 653777
Fax: 01823 216796
email: sales@halsgrove.com

An imprint of Halstar Ltd, part of the Halsgrove group of companies
Information on all Halsgrove titles is available at: www.halsgrove.com

Printed and bound in China by Toppan Leefung

Contents

How to use this book

Exmoor National Park is small and compact with a wonderful contrasting landscape of grass and heather moors, deep wooded combes, farmland and coastline, and many miles of clear sparkling streams, known as waters on Exmoor. It is not a wilderness landscape but one that has been shaped by people over thousands of years, a process still continuing today.

Exmoor like other national parks is a place where people both live and work but it is also open for recreation, so that the beauty, peace and tranquillity, can be enjoyed by those who seek them out. This small book of walks will, we hope, help those who visit Exmoor see some of the best of what is an area of outstanding natural beauty during their stay.

Reminders of how our ancestors lived worked and shaped the landscape can be seen with many archaeological historical and field system sites found on Exmoor.

Routes

The walks are graded from one to three boots — easy to more challenging. The walks are along way-marked public footpaths, bridleways, restricted byways, roads, old lanes (tracks) and permitted paths (paths where the owner has given permission for people to walk over their land but at the user's risk). The walks cross meadows, follow rivers, and cross some open access land, which belongs to the National Trust and the Exmoor National Park Authority. The walks pass through superb landscape with scenery of the highest merit with a rich variety of flora and fauna.

The Exmoor wildlife that may be seen on these walks includes the magnificent red deer that belong to the largest herd of wild deer outside of Scotland. Exmoor ponies run freely on the moor and are much admired and photographed. Other species to look out for include fox, badger, stoats, rabbits along with hares and goats. Buzzards, woodpeckers, dippers and grey wagtails are some of the many birds that might be seen along with pied flycatcher, redstart and a variety of woodland birds.

For botanical enthusiasts there are over a thousand species of flowering plants and grasses to discover.

Times and Distances

Times and distances quoted are approximate and are meant as a guide only but we hope that they will be of some help when planning your day. All the walks are circular so they start and finish at the same place. Some can be lengthened or shortened, therefore the miles quoted for each walk could alter considerably one way or the other. Where this is possible it is described in the route of the walk.

It is important that one has the right clothing and footwear along with an up to date map, whistle and compass.

Way Mark Colours
Footpath = Yellow
Bridleway = Blue
Restricted Byway = Purple

Map
Sketch maps are included, but they can only be a rough guide and OS maps are recommended. OS Outdoor Leisure 9 Exmoor.

Note
The routes of all the walks described, as far as the authors are aware, are correct and in regular use by the general public at the time of publication, including those that may not be

designated as public rights of way. Any person or persons using these suggested routes for a walk do so entirely at their own risk, as the authors and publishers do not accept responsibility or liability whatsoever for any injury or death under any circumstances or reasons to the said person or persons. Likewise no responsibility or liability can be accepted for those who trespass or do damage to land, crops or property however caused.

In conclusion we would like to say that although small and brief we hope that this small book will help to make your stay on Exmoor a happy and memorable one – take care and enjoy your walks.

Key to Symbols Used

Level of difficulty:

Easy 🍃

Fair 🍃 🍃

More challenging 🍃 🍃 🍃

Map symbols:

🚗 Park & start

Road

----- Footpath

■ Building / Town

+ Church

🍺 Pub

Text:

SP = signpost

Walk Locations

Hunters Inn **3**   **6** Valley of Rocks   **10** Brendon village   **1** Horner

EXMOOR NATIONAL PARK   **7** Dunster

Simonsbath **9**   **2** Exford

8 Winsford

Withypool **5**

Dulverton **4**

1 Horner

This is a very pleasant and easy walk that can be done at a leisurely pace and with the minimum of effort as most of the route is on level ground.

Horner is situated about a mile from Porlock. It is part of the Holnicote (pronounced Hunnicut) estate, once owned by the Acland family for two hundred years, which was given to the National Trust in 1944 by Sir Richard Acland, the 15th

Baronet. The cluster of houses, old mill and farm are set among green fields and woodland, with the clear, chattering Horner Water flowing peacefully nearby.

There is a good car park, public toilets and tea garden, combining to make this an ideal spot from which to explore this beautiful corner of the National Park. Many walks start from here, some leading through ancient woodland to the wild moor above.

Level:
Distance: 4-5 miles approx
Walking Time: 2-3 hours approx
Start & Finish: Car park
Public Toilets: Car park
Refreshments: Horner tea gardens (seasonal) and Porlock
Terrain: Meadows, lanes and road
Stiles: Yes
Grid Ref.: 899454

(map)

ossington
West Lynch
+
4
3
5 Packhorse Bridge
New Bridge
Allerford
2
Mill
6
West Luccombe
Holnicote House
Minehead
7
8
Burrowhayes
Horner
Wootton Courtenay
Horner Water
Webbers Post

Horner Cottages

into a field. Keeping close to the hedge on the left, continue on to reach a gate into a wood. Leave the wood by a kissing gate and continue ahead to a gate in a hedge. Cross two fields to join a road at a kissing gate.

Horner is a small hamlet that takes its name from the river which is thought to have derived from the old British word "Hwrnwr" meaning the snorer.

1 At the car park entrance turn right and walk along the road, keeping company with the bubbling Horner Water on your left. At the end of the caravan site on the left, look for the old packhorse bridge which crosses Horner Water. Continue along the road passing West Luccombe Farm – where the road bends sharp left go straight on to a gateway (SP A39 Road).

2 Cross the field to reach the road, turn right, at the end of the road bridge cross to a gate and go

Horner Water

*Bossington and Lynch,
Vale of Porlock*

Bossington village

3 There turn left along the road, to reach a bridge and SP on the right, (SP bridleway Selworthy Beacon). Before continuing cross the road to visit Lynch Chapel of Ease. After looking around the chapel, the walk can be lengthened with a short walk of just a few minutes to the pretty picture postcard village of Bossington.

At the birth of each of his nine children Sir Thomas Dyke Acland the tenth baronet commemorated the birth with a plantation of trees on the hill behind Allerford and Selworthy. Between the years of 1809 – 1826 over eight hundred thousand trees were planted.

4 Having visited Bossington retrace your steps back to the bridge, turn left across the bridge. Follow the bridleway up between buildings to reach a stony track. At the top of this turn right (SP footpath Allerford). Follow the path to the next SP there turn down right to Allerford. In a few minutes the path splits; keep right on lower path to join Aller Water before crossing the footbridge to reach a road junction.

Allerford packhorse bridge

11

5 At the road junction turn left, then walk through the village. On the way you pass the old thatched School House (now a rural museum well worth a visit), Old Smithy and a packhorse bridge, then turn right up to the main road. At the main road turn left. In a short distance cross the road and turn right into Piles Mill (NT worth looking round).

6 Follow the road up, leaving the mill on the left. Just past the mill, turn right up the bridleway (SP West Luccombe and Horner). At the junction of bridleways turn left, then continue until a stile is reached in the left hand hedge.

7 Here you have a choice — cross the stile and keep close to the hedge on the right, to reach another stile in the corner of the field, which rejoins the bridleway, or continue along the bridleway. (The bridleway does flood in very wet conditions.)

8 Cross a footbridge onto the road, turn left and walk back to the car park

Piles Mill

2 **Exford**

This lovely walk includes a long steep climb. However the beauty of the scenery throughout the walk more than compensates for the effort made to gain the top of the hill, where a fine view is the final reward.

The small village of Exford grew beside the ford that crossed the infant River Exe, as its name clearly implies. It lies in a valley and is set among soft green meadows and gentle hills — beyond these the landscape changes to become high windswept moorland.

Situated as it is in the heart of the Exmoor National Park, Exford is the ideal base to discover Exmoor and what it has to offer. Although small, Exford is often referred to as being the capital of the moor.

Level: 🥾 🥾
Distance: 6 miles approx
Walking time: 3-4 hours approx
Start & Finish: Exford car park
Public Toilets: Yes
Refreshments: The White Horse, The Crown Hotel and Chapel Tea Rooms
Terrain: Open moor, tracks, meadows, some road walking
Stiles: Yes
Grid ref.: 855384

13

Exford village

1 Walk to the gate at the end of the car park. Follow the path beside the River Exe until you reach a wide bridge at Court Farm. Turn left up a broad stony track SP Higher Combe, and Lyncombe. At the top of the track go over the stile on the right.

2 Keep close to the hedge on the left for the next three fields, in the corner of the third field

On the walk near Lyncombe

Below: *River Exe*

turn right to reach a gate in the fence. From this gate the path drops steeply to a bridge and a stile then climbs towards a house. At the gate opposite the house join a wide track and turn right SP Winsford.

3 Continue down the track and pass through a farm, the way ahead is along the valley bottom with hills rising steeply on each side. On reaching a SP (permitted bridleway) this could be taken to a footbridge over the River Exe.

Court Farm stands on the banks of the River Exe and was once a Methodist community. Parts of the house are reputed to be more than 500 years old.

Footbridge over
the River Exe

(4) Continue along the wide track to a sunken lane on the right and a SP bridleway Room Hill turn right down to a footbridge. From the footbridge the walk can be lengthened by following the riverside bridleway to

'The Harepath' an ancient track that once connected the Midlands to Cornwall forded the River Exe at Exford.

Nethercote Bridge and returning on the other side.

(5) Cross the footbridge and turn right, after a short distance at the end of a fence turn left onto a

View from Room Hill

track and then start the big climb up the side of Curr Cleave.

6 As you approach the top the path fades. Continue ahead and as you do angle slightly to the right along a path in the grass. Make your way across the flat top of Room Hill (can be difficult in mist).

7 When the head of a fenced off combe is reached keep to the left of it and bend to the right to arrive at a SP marked Withypool and Winsford.

8 Follow the track which goes straight at first then curves to the right around the head of a deep combe, continuing along a hedge on the left. Passing through some gates,

it then drops down hill to another gate and a SP Exford on the left.

9 Go through the gate. Cross the field to another gate that opens onto a track. Drop down to the valley bottom where the track leads

through more gates between fences and hedges to reach Court Farm. At Court Farm turn right, cross the bridge over the River Exe, then turn left and follow the riverside path back to the car park.

Looking towards Exford

3 **Hunters Inn**

This is a walk which has a lot of easy walking and many fine views, there is one steep climb and one or two lesser gradients.

Hunters Inn nestles in the beautiful Heddon Valley a quiet unspoilt corner of Exmoor. Today the Inn is popular with tourists who wish to stay in quiet country locations. Nearby there is a shop that is owned by the National Trust.

The National Trust own the Heddon Valley through which flows the lovely Heddon Water and they also protect the magnificent stretch of Exmoor coastline between Combe Martin and Woody Bay. The Heddon Valley is a mixture of woodland, small green meadows and steep scree-covered hillsides rising up hundreds of feet from the valley bottom. The scree was formed during the ice age.

Level: 🐾 🐾 🐾
Distance: 8-9 miles approx
Walking Time: 5-6 hours approx
Start & Finish: Car park
Public Toilets: Opposite car park
Refreshments: Hunters Inn, National Trust shop
Terrain: Lanes, woodland, meadows, coastpath, moorland and road
Stiles: No
Grid ref.: 655497

Heddon's Mouth

mbe

stone Hill
8

11

6

7   Moorland
    Cott

Trentishoe Down

be Martin

Trentishoe Lane

Rhydda Bank

Ladies
Mile

Hunters
Inn

River
Heddon

Trentishoe
Water

Hunters Inn nestles in the Heddon Valley

1. From the car park walk down the road passing the Inn on the right, follow the road until a gate is reached, just before the road bridge.

2. Turn left through the gate and follow the broad track until a four cross way of paths is reached SP. Turn right down the track, to a footbridge over Trentishoe Water. Cross this and turn left SP Ryhdda Bank.

Ladies Mile Footpath that starts at Rydda bank corner is a popular walk and one of the easiest on Exmoor.

3. When a SP marked Rhydda Bank and Trentishoe Mill is reached turn right uphill. On reaching a small tarmac road turn right for approximately 30 metres to join the main road. Turn left for approximately 60 metres to reach a SP, on the left marked Ladies Mile Footpath.

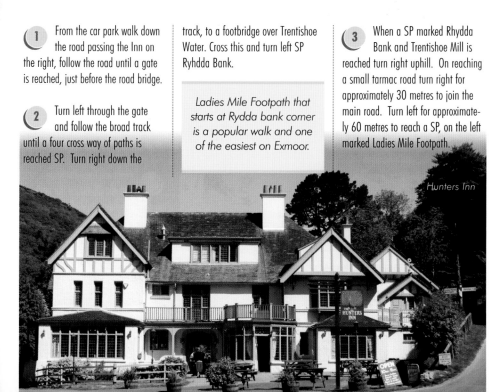

Hunters Inn

4 From the road follow the footpath as it threads its way beneath trees, on an elevated position. At a four cross way of paths SP, continue straight ahead along the path to another SP Holdstone Hill

5 Turn right and start the long climb to open moorland

reaching a post with a white arrow on it. The hardest part of the climb is now done; continue ahead from the post to arrive at a road.

6 At this point the walk can be shortened by turning right and walking past Moorland Cottage to a SP on left Coast Path. Turn left and

follow the wide track down to a SP on the right Coast Path.

7 Cross the road to a SP Holdstone Hill, Viewpoint 1146ft, follow the track to the top of Holdstone Hill which is marked with a large cairn.

8 From the cairn continue straight ahead on the path through the heather, with the large bulk of Hangman Hill in front of you. Where the path joins a stone wall keep it on your right and walk to a four cross way of paths.

9 From here turn right down hill to join the coast path through a gap in a wall SP, turn right and then in a short distance pass through

Ladies Mile Footpath

a gap in another wall. Ignore the path to the right and turn left down hill close to the wall, where the

ground levels out the path bends sharply to the right.

10 Continue along the broad track enjoying the easy walking, to arrive at a small path on the

View from Holdstone Hill

left and a marker post, coast path.

(11) Now follow the coast path signs until a triangle of paths is reached and a SP Coast Path and Trentishoe Church.

(12) Turn right and continue along by the wall until a road is reached in Trentishoe Combe.

(13) On reaching the road turn left down hill to join the main

Trentishoe church has a rare old minstrel's gallery and also contains a small organ from the RMS Mauretania that was presented by the Cunard Steam Ship Company in January 1966.

Hunters Inn road once again. For those with energy and time they may turn right and walk up the hill to visit the small but lovely Trentishoe church, then retrace their steps down the hill to the main road.

(14) At the main road, turn right for approximately 30 metres SP. Turn left and walk along the old lane to the bridge you crossed earlier. Cross the bridge and at the top of the slope turn left, and return to the Inn.

Heddon's Mouth from the Cleaves

4 **Dulverton**

This is a pleasant easy walk mainly across fields and through wooded combes, and follows part of an old railway line.

Dulverton lies deep in the valley of the beautiful River Barle surrounded by hills and woodland. There is a variety of accommodation and shops along with popular tea-rooms and inns. The Exmoor National Park offices are in Dulverton and there is a visitor's centre.

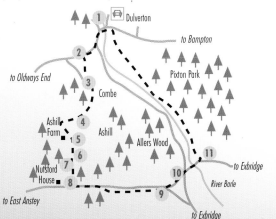

Level:
Distance: 4 miles approx
Walking time: 2-3 hours approx
Start & Finish: Exmoor House car park
Public Toilets: Yes
Refreshments: Dulverton
Terrain: Tracks, meadows, some road walking, old railway line
Stiles: Yes
Grid Ref.: 915280

Dulverton
Bridge

1. Leaving the car park entrance, turn left and walk to the main road, turn right and cross the bridge. Then cross the road and follow the tarmac path by the river. At the end of the path cross the road and walk up the hill SP Hawkridge. On rounding a corner lean on a gate to admire the view of Dulverton.

2. Cross the road to a stile go over and walk up the track to another stile and go into a field, keeping the trees on your left. Go up the field to reach a SP, pointing across the field to another SP, by a gate which gives access onto a farm lane.

3. Turn left, drop down and go through a gate to another gate on the right, SP footpath, cross the field. On reaching the bottom there is a sign pointing through a gate at the corner of a hedge, near a house. Cross the next bit of green diagonally to reach a SP and another gate, go through this and walk up the lower track, to reach another gate

The Aclands, Carnarvons, and Herberts are some of the great family names that have had connections with Dulverton.

Woodland footpath

Stile and waymark on walk

with a Public Footpath sign on the gate post.

4 Go through this gate and walk straight ahead across the field, keeping close to the hedge on the right. At the corner of the field turn left, and walk up the field to the top corner following the yellow markers on posts.

5 At this corner there is another footpath sign on the gate post, go through the gate and continue ahead close to the hedge that curves to the right. Just around the corner is another SP and gate.

6 Go through, continue ahead to a marker post near a gate then walk on to another marker post.

The Old Fish Wier, River Barle

Dulverton once had four active watermills; the buildings can still be seen today along with the mill leat.

There turn right to a third marker post and a SP a few metres ahead.

7 Here turn left and walk along the top of a field, keeping close to the hedge on the left. At the other end go through a gap in the hedge and walk down through the gorse bushes. The route is interspersed with yellow markers on posts for guidance.

River Barle
near Brushford

right and walk through the village to arrive at an off set crossroads SP Circular Walk.

(10) Cross the road, turn left then right and walk ahead to cross the River Barle, after which look for a stile and SP Dulverton Circular Walk, on the left. Cross the stile, and continue across the field to a gate and stile at the far end, go over the stile, cross a wide track and go through a kissing gate.

(8) On reaching the bottom SP Brushford Circular Walk, cross the stile and join the tarmac road. Go left and walk along the road, after about ten minutes look for a stile on the right, this is the way ahead. Cross another stile and turn left, follow the yellow markers; this is the old railway line.

(9) At the end of the railway section SP turn left down some steps, then go along a path to join the tarmac road SP Brushford. Turn

(11) The path now runs along by the river and is easy walking, eventually it leaves the river and threads its way through the buildings to join the main street, turn left and walk down to the bridge. Turn right and make your way back to the car park.

5 Withypool

This enjoyable walk which entails just two climbs to reach Winsford Hill, meanders through the beautiful Barle Valley.

Withypool village stands beside the lovely River Barle, which is spanned by a fine stone bridge. Like many of the Exmoor communities Withypool is not very big, but it still retains a shop, post office and a tea shop and gardens. A short distance away, is the church and the very popular Royal Oak Inn. There are cottages with small pretty gardens, and surrounding the village is a mixture of heather moors, woods and farmland.

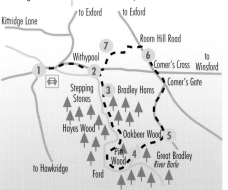

Level: ♥ ♥
Distance: 5.5 miles approx
Walking Time: 3-4 hours approx
Start & Finish: Car park
Public Toilets: In village
Refreshments: Tea gardens and pub
Terrain: Meadows, lanes, road and open moorland
Stiles: Yes
Grid Ref.: 845356

Withypool is an old Exmoor village. It takes it name from the willows or 'withies' that grow along the River Barle.

Withypool Bridge

(1) From the car park turn left and cross the fine stone bridge. Make your way through the village passing the village stores, the church and then the Royal Oak Inn, on your left. Continue on then, go up the hill until you reach a stile and SP on the right

(2) Go over the stile and walk along the path high above the River Barle. In a few metres it meanders through some trees, crosses a small stream and drops down to meet the river at a gate.

(3) After, the path follows the river bank and soon comes to some stepping stones across the river. Ignore these and continue on your way along the riverside path. This will lead you across meadows and through woodland.

Stepping stones across the River Barle

4 When a junction in the path, SP Winsford Hill, is reached, go left and walk up the track. After crossing a small ford go left at a SP marked avoiding farm. Climb the path to a small gate in a beech hedge

General Eisenhower visited Withypool's Royal Oak Inn during the Second World War whilst in the area.

Below Great Bradley

leading into a field. Keep close to the hedge on the right to reach another gate leading onto a tarmac lane. Turn left and continue uphill to a cattle grid.

5 Go through a gate next to a cattle grid and turn left. Follow the farm drive until another cattle grid is reached at Comer's Gate, on the main road to Exford. Turn left

at the cattle grid and walk up the road towards Exford, crossing the Winsford to Withypool road as you go.

6 On reaching the end of a post and wire fence, look for a SP and stile on the left in a beech hedge. Cross this and start making your way down the field towards Withypool, following the yellow signs.

7 On this part of the walk there will be good views of

Ford at Great Bradley

A stone circle on Withypool Hill indicates the presence of man in the area over many centuries.

Withypool Hill, Brightworthy Hill, the village below and the Barle Valley. As you go you will pass through several fields and cross some ladder stiles to eventually drop down a zig-zag path out onto the road. Turn right and make your way back to the car park.

Winsford Hill. Inset: Withypool

6 Valley of Rocks

A delightful walk this, made possible by the footpath that now goes around Crock Pits. This easy low level walk leaves the spectacular rock scenery of the Valley of Rocks and heads for Lee Abbey

The Valley of Rocks near Lynton has become a popular destination for tourists. The picturesque valley has wild goats and Exmoor ponies that never fail to attract the attention of visitors and their cameras.

The sculptured castellated rocks with names such as Ragged Jack and Castle Rock that give the valley its name are very impressive and well worth a visit to see.

Level: 🥾
Distance: 6-7 miles approx
Walking Time: 3-4 hours approx
Start & Finish: Valley of Rocks car park
Public Toilets: Picnic area
Refreshments: Lynton and Mother Meldrum's tea rooms (in the Valley of Rocks)
Terrain: Good paths, tracks, some road walking woodland and coastline
Stiles: Yes
Grid Ref.: 707497

to Woody Bay
Crock Point
Cuddy Cleave Wood
Crock Pits
Lee Abbey
Valley of Rocks
Castle Rock
View Point
to Lynton
Six Acre Wood
Six Acre Farm
to Croscombe Barton

35

The Valley of Rocks

1 Leave the car park and turn right then follow the small path running parallel to the road until a roundabout is reached; cross this to a SP on the right marked Coast Path. Continue up the road to a marked view point which is only a short distance on the right. Look at the White Lady at the top of Castle Rock; this is a silhouette among the rocks depicting a lady in a large bonnet and a long flowing dress carrying a basket.

A cave below a stack of rock known as the Devil's Cheesewring was the home of 'Mother Meldrum' a character in the book Lorna Doone. *This can be seen opposite Castle Rock.*

At the top of Castle Rock two large stones form a portal in the shape of what is known as the White Lady.

Right: *The White Lady*

Below: *The Devil's Cheesewring*

Lee Abbey, Lee and Woody Bay

 From here walk on to reach the gateway by a house, then continue on to the far end of Lee Abbey which is the tower gateway. Here turn left onto a wide track SP Six Acre Cross, and Lee Bay, with a very good view of Lee Bay from this point.

3 Go through the gate and follow the wide track, at the next junction of tracks SP Lee Bay, Crock Pits, continue ahead. The track soon enters some woodland where it then splits. Keep to the lower track and walk on to a bridge at the other end of a wide clearing under the trees; there is a small pond on the left by the bridge.

4 Cross the bridge and follow the track to the right, there is easy

Woodland waterfall

walking now, with a deep wooded gorge on the right. Just before a foot-bridge there is a SP on the right marked Lee Bay. The walk can be shortened here by turning right, to continue, walk on a few metres to the bridge SP Woodland Walk, Woody Bay.

Lee Abbey

(5) Turn right and cross the bridge then go up some stone steps opposite. This is a narrow track that threads its way through the trees for a short distance to join a bridleway SP Crock Pits. Cross the bridleway and continue up the path opposite. On joining the road SP Coast Path Woody Bay, turn left and walk up the road.

(6) After a few minutes a SP Lynton Coast Path, is reached on the right. Go down this and follow

the narrow path through the wood. When a stile is reached cross over it and turn left SP, then go left up two steps, turn right and go down to more steps.

(7) Continue ahead behind a tin shed to more steps there turn right through a gap in a hedge, then turn immediately left and continue along the path round the edge of the field crossing more stiles on the way. Eventually the path goes into some trees to reach a long flight of steps.

(8) On reaching the road, go left down hill and follow the road as it makes its way back to Lee Abbey and the gateway by the house once again.

(9) Here go left down the path by the gate pillar, at the bottom turn right where stunning views of the Valley of Rocks and particularly Castle Rock are seen. Continue along the path to rejoin the road; here go left to reach the roundabout then retrace your steps back to the car park.

7 Dunster

This is an excellent easy walk that should not be missed. After passing through the village an old pack horse bridge is crossed, then woodland tracks are followed to an outstanding view point high above the village.

Dunster is said to be one of the best medieval villages in the country.

Today numerous gift shops, tea rooms and galleries make Dunster a popular place to visit. There are many buildings of interest including St George's church, the castle and the Yarn Market. Above the village are Gallox Hill and Bat's Castle, settlements dating back to the Iron Age.

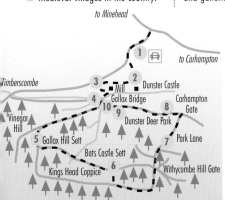

to Minehead
to Carhampton
Timberscombe
1
2 Dunster Castle
3 Mill
Gallox Bridge
4
10
8 Carhampton Gate
9
Vinegar Hill
Dunster Deer Park
5 Gallox Hill Sett
7 Park Lane
Bats Castle Sett
6
Kings Head Coppice
Withycombe Hill Gate

Level:
Distance: 5-6 miles approx
Walking time: 3-4 hours approx
Start and Finish: Dunster (main car park)
Public Toilets: Car park
Terrain: Parkland, tracks, hilltops, road and woodlands
Stiles: None
Grid Ref.: 990437

The Yarn Market, Dunster

1 Leave the car park by the top entrance and turn left. With the National Park Visitor Centre on your left, walk straight along the road into Dunster. Continue down the main street, passing the Yarn Market on your right. At the far end, walk through the gateway that leads to Dunster Castle.

2 Walk up the short slope to the National Trust shop and castle ticket office. Keeping these on your left, continue down the hill and pass through a gate to rejoin the main road. Turn left and continue until you reach the turning to Mill Lane on your left.

3 Walk down Mill Lane, with the leat on your left. Turn right at the signpost for Gallox Bridge. Cross the old pack horse bridge and continue ahead, passing some thatched cottages on the right. At the junction of paths, sign posted Dunster Woodland, Crown Estate, take the path marked Bat's Castle.

4 Continue up the hill, keeping left at the fork, following

Gallox Bridge Dunster

Looking down on Dunster

View from near Bat's Castle

signs for Bat's Castle. You will reach a three-way signpost at which point you turn left through the gate in the deer fence. Turn immediately right and continue steeply uphill – Gallax Hill Settlement will soon appear on your right.

(5) Continue along the path, which soon dips down, before rising gently to the Iron Age Bat's Castle Settlement, which will soon come into view on the skyline. Once reached stunning views can be enjoyed in all directions, including Dunster and Dunkery Beacon.

(6) After enjoying the views, continue straight along the path, passing a signpost on your left and slowly drop down to Withycombe Hill Gate. Go through the gate and turn left, following a wide track, flanked by a fine stone wall and sign posted Carhampton.

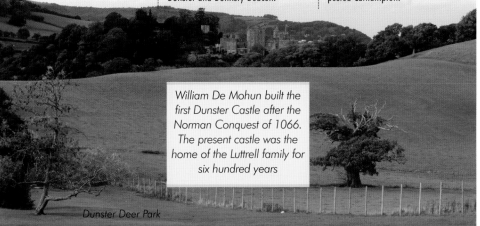

William De Mohun built the first Dunster Castle after the Norman Conquest of 1066. The present castle was the home of the Luttrell family for six hundred years

Dunster Deer Park

7 This track eventually passes an entrance to Wessex Water's underground reservoir, before reaching a crossway of tracks, Carhampton Gate. Turn left and go through the gate, following the track across the Deer Park to Dunster.

8 It will take you gently down past the old oak tree in the dip and on through another gateway. Continue on with the fence on your right and good views of the Castle and Conygar Tower.

9 The path leaves the fence and

At Dunster's old Frackford Bridge Mrs Alexander wrote the hymn 'All Things Bright and Beautiful'.

continues to contour the hillside before reaching a gate which brings you back to the Dunster Woodland Crown Estate sign that you passed at the start of the walk.

10 Turn right and follow the path back past the thatched cottages and over the pack horse bridge. From here retrace your steps back to the car park or extend your day with a visit to the mill, the castle or the shops!

Dunster Castle

8 Winsford

This walk involves a climb through woodland to reach the high moor, after its initial start from the village. After passing an ancient standing stone it threads its way through heather to reach the top of Winsford Hill, one of the finest viewpoints on Exmoor.

Winsford is often described as one of Exmoor's prettiest villages with its thatched inn 'The Royal Oak' and pack horse bridges. The War Memorial takes pride of place in the village's centre. There is a village hall, post office and shop, public toilets, and car park.

The lovely church of St Mary Magdalene has a tower standing, nearly 80ft high and has six bells.

Level: 🥾 🥾
Distance: 6-7 miles approx
Walking time: 4 hours approx
Start & Finish: Car park
Public Toilets: Near village hall
Refreshments: Bridge Cottage Tea Gardens (in season) and the Royal Oak Pub
Terrain: Moorland. tracks, paths and meadows
Stiles: Yes
Grid Ref.: 905350

Winsford

the path across what is known as the Allotment. Go up left after the gate

(4) Ahead now is a house known as 'Folly'. Near to this the path passes through a gate, after which, turn sharp left and keep by the hedge. As you do, look for a stone shelter on the right, a short distance

(1) Follow the road past the War Memorial, then The Royal Oak Inn. Go left along a bridleway SP Winsford Hill to arrive at a footbridge across a stream near Yellow Combe cottage.

(2) Cross the bridge and follow the bridleway (SP) to the top of Yellow Combe, to reach a gate into a field, go through this and turn right (SP) for Spire Cross.

(3) Walk by the hedge on the right. In a corner you come to a small gate, ignore this and go on to another gate a few metres up the hedge. Go through the gate and follow

Along the bridleway

away, under which will be the Caractacus Stone.

 From the stone, go ahead about 200 metres to reach Spire Cross. Continue along the Knaplock road for about 300 metres and turn right onto a wide track used by horses. Follow it up the hillside. When it starts to level out, look for a wide distinct path through the heather coming in from the right, at a four crossway of tracks.

 Turn right along this path to reach the road — cross it and walk straight on to arrive at the Wambarrows and the top of Winsford Hill, at 1,404 ft. Dartmoor, the Blackdown Hills, Dunkery and Withypool Hills can all be seen in favourable conditions.

7 From the trig-point pillar take

On Winsford Hill that rises 1,404 feet above the village are Bronze Age mounds known as the Wambarrows, an excellent view point.

One of the Wambarrows, Winsford Hill

a wide path to the right of it from your way of approach. This leads to an even broader track that bears to the right. Follow this down to the edge of the Punch Bowl a natural amphitheatre in the side of Winsford Hill.

8 From the top of the Punch Bowl go left, first along the top edge of it and then down the left hand side of it. Near the bottom a gate leads into a field (Blue Mark). Keep close to the hedge on your right until another gate is reached.

9 Go through this and then keep close to the hedge on your left. On reaching a third gate, follow the track through the farm. At the farm gate, look for a SP yellow mark on the right. This marks the footpath back to Winsford along the bottom of some fields (dogs on leads).

View from Winsford Hill.

The Caractacus stone is one of only three inscribed stones on Exmoor.

The Punch Bowl is an impressive two hundred feet deep natural amphitheatre in the side of Winsford Hill.

Looking up the Punch Bowl

10 The path leads through gateways, and then enters a sunken lane behind some houses. At the end of the lane, the road is soon reached. Walk down the road to the village passing the Church.

11 Nearing the bottom of the hill, look for an opening between the cottages on the right. This leads to an old packhorse bridge and a small gate, which you enter to cross some grass and a footbridge. Turn left and walk back to the car park.

The Winn Valley

9 Simonsbath

This is a pleasant walk with very little uphill involved.

Early records of 1540, show that at the spot where Simonsbath village now stands, there was just a crossway of tracks over wild moorland with a wooden bridge spanning the River Barle. Simonsbath can be considered a young village as it only developed from the eighteen hundreds. In the village of Simonsbath today there are two hotels, a restaurant named after James Boevey, and a church.

Level: 🥾
Distance: 4 miles approx
Walking Time: 3 hours approx
Start & Finish: Car park
Public Toilets: Car park
Refreshments: Boevey's Resturant and The Exmoor Forest Hotel
Terrain: Grass moorland, woodland, and meadows
Stiles: Yes
Grid ref.: 775394

1 Walk to the SP Preyway Head in the upper car park. Follow the path through the trees to an open area. Turn down left with a fence on the right. Crossing a stream go through the trees and a gate into a field.

2 Cross the field following the marker posts (yellow) to a gate in a fence, go through turn right and follow the path to a wall. Turn left now and cross a board walk over wet ground to reach a footbridge.

3 A few metres after the foot-bridge turn right SP, and meander up through the rushes and grass following the marker posts and crossing another footbridge.

4 On arriving at a gate in a

Simonsbath

walled bank SP Preyway Head, Warren Farm, turn left and cross the field to join a road. Turn right and walk along the road, to a lay by on the corner which is Preyway Head (SP permitted bridleway to Exe Head).

5 Go through the gate, turn right and follow the track for a few metres then turn right to a gate and SP bridleway, go through the gate turn left and walk ahead with first a hedge and then a fence on the

Infant River Exe at Preyway Head

1654 was the year James Boevey completed the first house to be built in the Royal Forest.

left. At the end of the fence SP bridleway turn left to a gate go down the next field close to hedge on the left to a gate next to a sheep pen SP.

6 Go through the gate and turn right walk ahead towards the next gate. Just before you reach it, turn left and walk down the field to arrive at a small gate in a corner SP bridleway — Lime Combe cottage can be seen in front of you.

7 With Lime Combe below on

River Barle, Simonsbath

River Barle and reflections of Simonsbath House Hotel

the left, cross the next field to a small gate in a hedge SP bridleway. From here make your way ahead passing around the head of a small side combe. Continue along the edge of Lime Combe until a gate is reached, go through this and turn left into a wood SP (there are three large stones nearby) and follow the marker poles.

8 At the end of the wood SP, turn left down a wide track,

then go through a gate to join a disused road SP, walk ahead to the main road. Cross the road and turn left for approx 30 metres to a SP footpath to Simonsbath.

9 Turn right down the wide track to a gate SP, turn left and then cross a stile to a board walk. At the end of that cross the footbridge and keeping close to a wall on the left walk ahead a few metres to a gap in the wall.

10 Turn left through this, then follow the obvious path through fields and over stiles with the leat below on the right to arrive at a footbridge behind the sawmills. Cross this to a SP and footbridge then join the road next to Simonsbath bridge; turn left here and walk up to the junction, turn right and walk up through the village to reach the car park.

Left: *Late evening at Limecombe*

John Knight purchased 10,000 acres of the Royal Forest known as the 'Kings Allotment' for fifty thousand pounds. He then had a 29 mile long wall built around his estate, which can still be seen today.

Ashcombe Water

10 Brendon village

This walk offers a good day out on foot. Part of the walk is beside the lovely East Lyn River. An excellent walk in our opinion and one not to miss if in the area.

Below the A39 Lynton to Porlock road is Brendon village. It is in a long narrow valley with steep sided hills rising up on both sides. Keeping the village company is the East Lyn River which flows through the valley on its way to embrace the sea at Lynmouth. The surrounding countryside is a mixture of woodland, green fields and moorland. Brendon has a nice village hall, car park and toilets and the popular Staghunters Inn. Brendon church stands high on a hill two miles from the village.

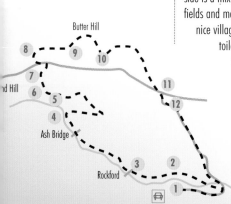

Level: 🐾 🐾 🐾
Distance: 6-7 miles
Walking Time: 5-6 hours approx
Start & Finish: Brendon village hall
Toilets: Car park
Refreshments: Staghunters Inn and Rockford Inn
Terrain: Tracks, footpaths, road walking, woodland, and moorland
Styles: No
Grid Ref.: 768484

Car park and village hall, Brendon

① Leave the car park turn left, walk through the village to Leeford Green. Turn left here and cross the bridge, turn left again for a short distance to a wide track on the left and a SP public footpath

The old Staghunters Inn has one room that was once a chapel and is reputed to be haunted.

Rockford, Watersmeet. Follow the track then go through a gate marked Countisbury Mill.

② At the mill go through a gate and follow the obvious riverside path to a footbridge with the hamlet of Rockford with its seventeenth century inn on the other side of the river.

'Long pool', one of many attractive pools found along the course of the East Lyn River, is favoured by fishermen.

East Lyn River at Leeford

3 From the bridge, continue along the riverside path to reach Ash Bridge continue ahead a short distance to a SP (Countisbury) on the right.

4 This is the start of the climb

Riverside path

Ash Bridge

up to Countisbury. At a sharp bend in the path, SP (Countisbury), turn left up a long flight of steps, at the top continue along the path as it rises and falls gently through woodland.

5 Arriving at a four crossway of paths SP Winston's Path, Countisbury, continue ahead. After some steps and a gate Wind Hill with its impressive defence works comes into view.

6 Below is seen Myrtleberry where the river sweeps around it in a large bend. As it nears its end the path drops down to the head of Chistle Combe and a pond. On the right is a SP Lynmouth.

Wind Hill Iron Age
Defence Works

Wind Hill has impressive defensive ramparts and dates back to the Iron Age. It can be seen near Countisbury.

7 Go left now and walk by the pond and walk up the slope to a gate next to the main road. Cross the road, to a SP permitted path, Coast Path, Lynmouth. Follow the path to a gate and enter a field. From the gate walk up by a wall on the right, when the wall curves around to the right a SP (Coast Path Lynmouth) will be seen up on the top of the wall.

8 From there continue ahead and follow the wall to reach Countisbury church. At the church angle to the left and walk to a corner of a wall.

9 From the corner of the wall a narrow path can be seen on the left threading its way up a short distance to reach the top of Butter Hill. When ready to leave turn right at the trig point and follow the wide grass path back to the wall turn left, and walk to the entrance of Barna Barrow car park.

10 From Barna Barrow go left along a wide track which curves to the right. When you reach a junction of tracks keep straight on and then do the same at the next two junctions to reach a small tarmac road and a SP Kipscome. There turn right and follow it to the main road.

11 On reaching the main road, cross over onto the grass and turn left. Walk ahead to a cattle grid and go through the gate next to it, continue to a road junction SP Brendon.

12 Turn right here and follow the road back to Brendon, retracing your steps back through the village to the car park — tired legs but a small price to pay for an excellent walk.

Coastal view of Lynton and Lynmouth